Breaking Free

from

Condemning Thoughts

TERESA LEGATES

ISBN 979-8-89043-388-6 (paperback)
ISBN 979-8-89043-389-3 (digital)

Christian Faith Publishing
832 Park Avenue
Meadville, PA 16335
www.christianfaithpublishing.com

Printed in the United States of America

Contents

Preface

Searching for answers to why you feel different from others? Are you dealing with shame, guilt, and shyness, feel unworthy of God's love, or unable to forgive yourself? Chances are, self-condemnation is to blame. Prayerfully read each page, asking God to open hearts and minds to the truth of his word, bringing freedom from such condemning thoughts.

Where Condemnation Originated

What is condemnation? According to the *Merriam-Webster Dictionary*, condemnation is "the action of condemning someone to a punishment, pass sentence on, and find guilty." There is no better place to bring the message of condemnation out into the light of day than where it all began.

In Genesis 1:27–6:13,

> So God created man in his own image. He commanded they could eat of the trees of the garden but not the tree of the knowledge of good and evil, for in the day they eat of it they would surely die. They were both naked and were not ashamed.
>
> The serpent (Satan) comes to Eve with questions about what God commanded, to pull Eve into a conversation with him; Eve fell for it hook, line and sinker. Eve responded, "We can eat the fruit of the garden but not the fruit of the tree of knowledge of Good and Evil, neither touch it, lest we die."

Satan, as sly as he is, tells Eve that she will not surely die: "For God knows that when you do eat of the tree of the knowledge of good and evil, you will be like God knowing good and evil." Satan planted the seed of doubt about God's faithfulness by claiming God is holding something good back from them. The truth is found in God's Word.

> For the Lord God is a sun and shield, the
> Lord will give Grace and Glory. No good thing
> will be held from them that walk uprightly.
> (Psalm 84:11 KJV)

Eve, leaning on her own understanding, starts doubting God's faithfulness, thinking God is holding something good back from them. She looks at the tree of the knowledge of good and evil; she sees it is good for food and pleasant to the eyes. Its fruit could make them wise and be like God.

She partakes of the fruit, gives it to Adam, and they both eat. Both their eyes open to the knowledge of good and evil. Seeing their nakedness, they sewed fig leaves together to cover their shame.

Hearing the voice of God walking in the garden, they quickly tried to hide themselves from the presence of God. God called out to Adam, "Where are you?"

Adam said, "I heard your voice and I was afraid. Because I am naked, I hid myself."

God said, "Who told you that you were naked? Have you eaten of the tree that I commanded you not to eat?"

Adam blames Eve, while Eve blames the serpent (Satan).

Let us take a look at what has taken place here. God gave Adam and Eve an authoritative order (command) not to eat of the tree of the knowledge of good and evil. The minute Adam and Eve took from the tree, their eyes were opened to the knowledge of their sin, the sin of disobedience, thus condemning them to death (spiritual death, separation from God).

> Yes, Adam's One sin brings condemnation
> for everyone, but Christ's one act of righteous-
> ness brings a right relationship with God and
> new life for everyone. (Romans 5:18 NLT)

> God did not give the law to live by to make one holy. He gave the law so we could see our need for him.

> Wherefore the law was our Schoolmaster to bring us unto Christ, that we might be justified by faith. (Galatians 3:24 KJV)

> Therefore, no one will be declared righteous in God's sight by the works of the law; rather, through the law we become conscious of our sin. (Romans 3:20)

Justification is God's righteous act of removing the guilt and penalty of sin while declaring the ungodly to be righteous through faith (or trust) in Christ's atoning sacrifice.

> Whoever believes in him is not condemned, but whoever does not believe, stands condemned already, because they have not believed in the name of God's one and only son. (John 3:18 NIV)

> If we confess our sins, he is faithful and just to forgive us of our sins and to cleanse us from all unrighteousness. (1 John 1:9 NKJV)

Cleansing is God's gift to us; God's gift that was paid for by the precious blood of Jesus. God is faithful to forgive and cleanse us from all unrighteousness. One must remember, we do not cleanse ourselves, nor earn cleansing. God cleanses us for his sake; he is a holy God.

> I, I am he who blots out your transgressions for my own sake, and I will not remember your sins. (Isaiah 43:25 ESV)

Jesus took our sins onto himself, he canceled the record of the charges against us and took it away by nailing it to the cross. (Colossians 2:14 NLT)

There is therefore now no condemnation to them who put their trust in Christ Jesus. (Romans 8:1 KJV)

Now if we do sin, we have an advocate.

My dear children, I write this to you so you will not sin, but if anybody does sin, we have an advocate with the father, Jesus Christ, the righteous one. He is the atoning sacrifice for our sins, and not only for our sins, but for the sins of the world. (1 John 2:1–2)

Struggling with Thoughts of Condemnation

After all Christ has done for us, why do we still struggle with feelings of condemnation?

The condemnation we are now feeling is not from God. When we believe the lies of the enemy of our souls, we experience self-condemnation.

> Self-condemnation – the act or an instance
> of condemning one's own character or actions,
> very strongly disapproves of oneself; also believes
> God very strongly disapproves.

We beat ourselves up over sin in our lives, trying to pay the price Christ has already paid. It is as if we believe that self-condemnation helps pay the price for our sins, somehow making it more forgivable by suffering for it. In a sense, we are saying Christ's sacrifice was not enough. We continue punishing ourselves with condemning thoughts.

Self-condemnation is the enemy's tool that he uses to keep us in bondage, keeping us from communion with God. Notice that God does not place a wedge between us and him; our sin and condemning thoughts stand in the way. Satan is behind all these shenanigans (dishonest activity). Satan's tactic is self-condemnation. When we believe the condemning lies, we are defeated.

> And I heard a loud voice saying in heaven,
> now is come salvation, and strength, and the

kingdom of our God, and the power of his Christ; for the accuser of our brethren is cast down, which accused them before God day and night. (Revelation 12:10 KJV)

Satan is the accuser of the brethren (those who put their trust in Christ), accusing them before God day and night. The Hebrew word for Satan, *hassatan*, means "prosecutor at law" or "accuser." The role of prosecutor is to condemn, to bring up all the dirt he can on someone. Satan relentlessly accuses until one feels condemned.

I can almost hear the condemning lies the enemy perhaps may have been whispering to Adam and Eve, trying to keep them under self-condemnation.

Conviction or Self-Condemning Thoughts

Many years I lived with self-condemnation, believing all the lies the enemy whispered to me and believing they were coming from a judgmental God, waiting for me to mess up to call down judgment. So far from the truth about who God is! God seeks to extend his love and care for us by sending his son, Jesus, to die for us to make things right with God so we can have a personal relationship with him.

> He spared not his own son, but delivered
> him up for us all, how shall he not with him also
> freely give us all things. (Romans 8:32 KJV)

You see, God held nothing back to bring us into a relationship with him. Conviction says God will help you; condemnation says there is no hope for you.

Conviction is a by-product or fruit of a relationship with God. God speaks to our hearts as we read his Word, hear his Word preached, and listen to other believers. The Holy Spirit lets us know when we have sinned (the act of going against God and his ways, disobedience). We feel a prick in our inner being, our hearts and our souls. The Holy Spirit lets us know immediately that communion with God has been broken. There is dread in our souls upon seeing how our sin dishonors God. We cry out in repentance, with great desire to be back in communion with God. We seek to live in obedience that pleases God out of the love we have for him, not obligation.

Let us now take a look at a heart under conviction.

Peter's Conviction, Matthew 26:69–27:14

The night Jesus was arrested, he was taken before the high priest. Peter, sitting outside in the courtyard, is approached by a servant girl, who pointed Peter out as one of those with Jesus the Galilean. Peter denied it: "I don't know what you're talking about."

Later by the gate, another servant girl noticed Peter and said to those around her, "This man was with Jesus of Nazareth." Again, Peter denied Christ: "I don't even know the man." A little later, a bystander spoke out, saying to Peter, "You must be one of them. We can tell by your Galilean accent." Peter swore an oath: "A curse on me if I am lying—I don't know the man!" Immediately, the rooster crowed. Suddenly, Jesus's words flashed through Peter's mind and heart: "I tell you, Peter, before the rooster crows today, you will deny three times that you know me."

Peter immediately felt conviction as his communion with God had been broken. He could see how he dishonored Christ through betrayal. Peter cries out bitterly, yearning to be back in communion with Christ out of love and not obligation.

Example: David cries out to God as he is under conviction.

> For I acknowledge my transgressions, and my sin is always before me. Against you, you only, have I sinned, and done evil in your sight. That you may be found just when you speak, and blameless when you judge. (Psalm 51:3–4 NKJV)

> Create in me a clean heart, oh God, and renew a steadfast Spirit within me. (Psalm 51:10 NKJV)

> If we confess our sins, he is faithful and just to forgive us our sins and to cleanse us from all unrighteousness. (1 John 1:9 NKJV)

Conviction draws us back to God, offering us a remedy, repentance, life, and freedom.

Judas's Self Condemnation, Matthew 27:3–5

Judas, who betrayed Jesus, was filled with remorse (guilt for a wrong committed). Judas tried to silence his guilt by returning the thirty pieces of silver to the leading priest and the elders. He told them that he has sinned and betrayed an innocent man. They retorted, "Why do we care? That's your problem." Judas tried to clear the wreckage up by himself. He threw the silver coins down in the temple and went out and hung himself.

Self-condemnation says there is no hope.

Antidote to Satan's Lies and Deception

Knowing God's truth is the antidote to Satan's lies and deceptions. We must search the scriptures to know the truth. Here are a few examples:

Fear sets in, and one fears there is no hope.

> Fear not, for I am with you. Be not dismayed, for I am your God. I will strengthen you, Yes, I will help you. I will also uphold you with my righteous right hand. (Isaiah 41:10 NKJV)

Satan whispers, "God will not forgive you."

> I, even I, am He who blots out your transgressions for my own sake; and I will not remember your sins. (Isaiah 43:25 NKJV)

When Satan whispers, "God will not forgive you this time. You already confessed that before, and you went right back to it. What makes you think he will forgive you this time?"

> If we confess our sins, He is faithful and just to forgive us of our sins and to cleanse us from all unrighteousness. (1 John 1:9 KJV)

When Satan whispers, "Surely someone else is more suited to do God's work than you."

For it is God who is working in you both to will and to work according to his good purpose. (Philippians 2:13 CSB)

Good News!

As Romans 8:1 says, paraphrased: "There is therefore now no condemnation to those who put their trust in Christ Jesus."

We no longer have to live with self-condemnation. Jesus paid it all in full. We talked about taking God's truth (word of God) and using it as an antidote against Satan's lies. First, we must understand what we are up against. Knowing the truth helps us to see clearly what the enemy is up to. However, mentally knowing the truth is not enough. One must take action, taking God's word and defending themselves from the lies of the enemy. Paul tells us in Ephesians 6:13 to put on every piece of God's armor, so we will be able to resist the enemy in the time of evil. Then, after the battle, we will be standing firm.

Putting on the Armor of God

Let us now go through each piece of armor—what it is, how to apply it, and how to use it.

Below is the armor of God, as explained in Ephesians 6:13–18:

Belt of truth:

> Declare God's word.
> Speak truth, resisting Satan's attacks.

Breastplate of righteousness:

> Live in obedience to God.
> Showing faith and love brings honor to his name.

Shoes of peace:

> Stand firm in the truth of God's word and
> who God says we are.
> Sharing God's truth with others strengthens us.

Shield of faith:

> Confidently trust in who God is.
> Confidently trust in God's promises.
> Take God at his word regardless of circumstances.

Helmet of salvation:

> Focus on Christ, his plan and purpose.
> Focus thoughts on who we are in Christ.

Sword of the spirit:

> Speak the word of God against the lies of the enemy.

Prayer:

> Ask God for wisdom to use his word effectively to fight off the enemy.
> Seek to know God.
> Praise God for his protection and faithfulness.

Areas Affected by Self-Condemnation

Ready to fight back? Now we know what self-condemnation is, where it came from, and who we are up against. Knowing we are not defenseless with God's armor, we must now dive into the areas of our lives that are most affected by self-condemnation or condemning thoughts.

1. Torturous thoughts about the past
2. Self unforgiveness
3. Thoughts of unworthiness
4. Judgmental and critical spirit

Torturous Thoughts about the Past

Thoughts seem to creep up from the past, causing one to live the pain over and over again. Recalling those memories leaves us feeling perhaps shameful, full of guilt, and not good enough. These are all self-condemning thoughts. Let us now take back ground the enemy has stolen.

Taking back ground the enemy has stolen

1. Take each thought captive.

> Casting down imaginations, and every high thing that is exalted against the knowledge of God, and bringing every thought into captivity

to the obedience of Christ. (2 Corinthians 10:5 ERV)

When a condemning thought comes, stop it dead in its tracks. Speak out loud, "No, I do not live in the past. Jesus has made all things new. Jesus has paid it all. I am living in the present, looking at what God is doing in my life right now."

> Remember not the former things, neither consider the things of old [forget the past]. Behold, I am doing a new thing; Now it springs forth, do you not perceive it? I will make a way in the wilderness and rivers in the desert. (Isaiah 43:18–19 ESV)

> In all your ways acknowledge him and he will make straight your path. (Proverbs 3:6 ESV)

2. Stop allowing ourselves to replay bad choices and bad experiences.

3. Make a decision to leave the past in the past and focus on the here and now.

Self unforgiveness

Do you find it easier to forgive others than yourself? Have you been beating yourself up over bad choices, sins of the past? Are you dealing with deep shame, guilt, and mental torment over what you should not have done, should have done, could have done? Feelings of defeat are holding you hostage, prohibiting you from moving forward. All these condemning thoughts are lies that we are not truly delivered.

> Therefore, there is now no condemnation for those who are in Christ Jesus. (Romans 8:1 NIV)

Remember, the enemy wants to keep us in bondage through self-condemnation. We must turn to the Word of God to know the truth.

Let us go back to the garden, where it all began.
In Genesis 3:5–6,

> For God knows that on the day you eat of it [tree of knowledge of good and evil] your eyes will be opened, and you will be like God, knowing good and evil.

Eve, leaning on her own logic, sees the tree is good for food, that it is pleasant to the eyes and a tree to be desired to make one wise. She partook of the fruit thereof. Eve began to doubt God's truthfulness, thinking God is holding something good back from them.

It is so important not to lean on our own understanding or logic.

> Trust in the Lord with all your heart and lean not on your own understanding. In all your ways acknowledge him and he shall direct your paths. (Proverbs 3:5–6 NKJV)

We must turn to the word of God to know the truth, not lean on our own understanding.

> Thy word is true from the beginning and every one of thy righteous judgments endureth forever. (Psalm 119:160 KJV)

> Therefore, if any man be in Christ, he is a new creature [person]. Old things have passed away; behold all things have become new. (2 Corinthians 5:17 KJV)

> Forget the former things; do not dwell on the past. See I am doing a new thing [in your life]. Now it springs up; do you not perceive it? I'm making a way in the wilderness and streams in the wasteland. (Isaiah 43:18–19 NIV)

> For as the heaven is high above the earth, so great is his Mercy toward them that [put their trust in him] fear him. As far as the east is from the west, so far has he removed our transgressions from us. (Psalm 103:11–12 KJV)

Christ has forgiven us. So why should we not forgive ourselves?

Ready to forgive myself?

For us to be able to forgive ourselves, we must renew our minds to think and speak truth. The truth is God's Word:

> Sanctify [cleanse] them through your truth: your word is truth. (John 17:17 KJV)

> If so be that you have heard him, and have been taught by him, as the truth is in Jesus: that you put off concerning the former conversation [Greek: *anastrophin*, meaning behavior, conduct] which is corrupt according to the deceitful lust; and be renewed in the spirit of your mind. And that you put on the new man [new way of living], which after God is created in righteousness and true holiness. Wherefore putting away lying, speak every man truth. (Ephesians 4:21–25 KJV)

Renew our minds to think and speak truth

1. Take thoughts captive.
   No longer speak the lies of self-condemning thoughts.

   Casting down imaginations, and every high thing that is exalted against the knowledge of God, and bringing every thought into captivity to the obedience of Christ. (2 Corinthians 10:5 ASV)

   Holding thoughts up to the truth of God's Word. Tearing down strongholds that have built themselves up in our minds against the truth. By speaking the truth, we block the lies that are trying to make their way from our minds to our hearts.

2. Guard our hearts by hanging on to the truth of God's Word.

   Keep thy heart with all diligence for out of it are the issues of life. (Proverbs 4:23 KJV)

3. Recognize self-focus.
   Self-focus is having self-defeating thoughts.

4. Focus on God.

   You keep him in perfect peace whose mind stays [focused] on you, because he trusts you. (Isaiah 26:3 ESV)

5. Seek God's direction.

   Trust In the Lord with all your heart, and lean not on your own understanding; in all your ways acknowledge him, and he shall direct your paths. (Proverbs 3:5–6 NKJV)

6. Rest in Christ.
Rest in the truth of God's word. Come to Christ through prayer.

Come to me, all of you who are weary and loaded down with burdens, and I will give you rest. (Matthew 11:28 ISV)

7. Put on the armor of God.
Put on the armor of God to be able to stand ground during attacks from the enemy.
When we fall short of the mark, we confess our sins, turn from them, and receive cleansing from Christ.

If we confess our sins, He is faithful and just to forgive us our sins and to cleanse us from all unrighteousness. (1 John 1:9 ESV)

Note: God is the one who does the cleansing, not us.

Six Godly Men Who Struggled with Thoughts of Unworthiness

Peter, John 13:2–11 KJV

Jesus was alone with his disciples in the upper room the night of the last supper. Jesus rose up from supper, and laid aside his garments: [Jesus laid aside who he is, Lord of lords, King of kings and became a servant]. Taking a towel and girded himself, he poured water into a basin and began to wash the disciples' feet, wiping them with the towel he had wrapped around him.

When Jesus came to Simon Peter, Peter said, "Lord, are you going to wash my feet?"

Jesus answered and said to Peter, "What I do you know not now, but you will know here after."

Peter, of his own impulsive will, pulled his feet back and said to Jesus, "You will never wash my feet."

Peter refused to be cleansed by Jesus. He thought he was showing humility by refusing to have his feet washed by Christ, but in truth, it was pride. Peter was focused on himself, finding it hard to lay aside who he was. Jesus answered Peter, "If I wash you not, you have no part with me [will not belong to me]."

Christ forgives us of our sins for his sake.

> I, even I, am He who blots out your transgressions for my own sake; and I will not remember your sins. (Isaiah 43:25 NKJV)

> Let this mind be in you, which was also in Christ Jesus: Who, being in the form of God, thought it not robbery to be equal with God; But made himself of no reputation, and took upon him the form of a servant, and was made in the likeness of men: And being found in fashion as a man, he humbled himself, and became obedient unto death, even the death of the cross. (Philippians 2:5–8 KJV)

Many times, we miss out on all God has for us, we see ourselves as unworthy to be cleansed by a holy God, thereby refusing God's goodness. There is no need to feel unworthy—it is not about us; it is all about him. May we learn to accept the love of Christ humbly and be cleansed by his power.

Those who are dealing with thoughts of unworthiness may be listening to the thoughts of self-condemnation. Thoughts of blame, guilt, shame, unworthiness, being unable to forgive oneself, being not good enough, etc.—God's word tells us how to stop these unwanted foes.

> Take every thought captive using God's mighty weapons, the whole armor of God [truth, righteousness, peace, faith, who we are in Christ, the word of God, and prayer], to tear down the strongholds of human reasoning [logic] and to destroy every proud obstacle that keeps people from knowing God. We capture rebellious thoughts and teach them to obey Christ.

Mephibosheth, 2 Samuel 9:1–13

Mephibosheth was the son of Jonathan and grandson of King Saul of Israel. Saul was jealous of David, who killed the giant Goliath, so much that he proposed in his heart to kill him. David and Jonathan were very best of friends. As the story goes, King Saul and Jonathan both died in the battle of Mount Gilboa. David then became king of Israel. David purposed in his heart to show kindness to the House of Saul for Jonathan's sake.

David called for Saul's servant, Ziba. David asked Ziba if there was anyone left of the House of Saul that he may show the kindness of God to him. Ziba tells David about Jonathan's son Mephibosheth, who is crippled in both his feet. David calls for Mephibosheth to be brought before him. Mephibosheth falls on his face in reverence to David. He said, "Behold your servant."

David said, "Fear not, for I will surely show you kindness for your father, Jonathan, and will restore you all the land of your grandfather Saul, and you shall eat at my house continually."

Mephibosheth bowed and exclaimed, "Who am I that you should look upon such a dead dog as I am?"

David declares that Mephibosheth shall eat bread always at his table as one of his sons. So Mephibosheth lived in Jerusalem and continually ate at the king's table, even though he was lame in both his feet.

So we see it is not about whether we are worthy. It is about God's goodness, bringing glory to his name. We could never earn a place at the table.

Gideon, Judges 6:1–16

Gideon, son of Joash the Abiezrite, was down by the winepress, threshing wheat to hide it from the Midianites. As the story goes, the Israelities did evil and would not repent, so God gave them over to the hands of the Midianites for seven years. Thereby, the Israelites became poverty-stricken.

The Israelites cried out to God. God, in his great mercy, sent his angel of the Lord (Jesus) to appear to Gideon, declaring, "The Lord is with you, thou mighty man of valor. Go in your might, and you shall save Israel from the hand of the Midianites. Have I not sent you?"

Gideon, struggling with thoughts of unworthiness (not good enough, etc.), cried out, "Oh, my Lord, how shall I save Israel? Look at me, my family is poor in Manasseh, and I am the least in my father's house."

The Lord proclaimed, "Surely, I will be with you, and you will kill the Midianites as if they were one man."

Gideon might have thought, *I'm the last person anyone would even consider being able to save Israel out of the hands of the Midianites.* He saw himself as unworthy, not good enough; God saw him as a mighty man of valor.

> Gideon and his army of 300 men killed the Midianites as if they were one man. (Judges 7:16–25)

> Then the men of Israel said unto Gideon, "Rule thou over us, both thou and thy son, and thy son's son also; for thou has delivered us from the hand of Midian." And Gideon said unto them, "I will not rule over you, neither shall my

son rule over you: the Lord shall rule over you."
(Judges 8:22–23 KJV)

Gideon discovered that it is all about God's grace and that he will never be good enough without it.

> God, who gives life to the dead and calls those things which do not exist as though they did. (Romans 4:17 NKJV)

> And he said unto me, "My grace is sufficient for you, for my strength is made perfect in weakness." (2 Corinthians 12:9 KJV)

It is not about us—it is all about God, who does the work in us and through us as we submit to him.

> For it is God who works in you both to will and to do for His good pleasure. (Philippians 2:13 NKJV)

John the Baptist, John 1:6–8, 15, 27

Through John the Baptist, we will see unworthiness born out of humility instead of self-focus pride.

John the Baptist was born to Zacharias, the priest, and Elisabeth in their old age. An angel appeared to Zacharias while he was in the temple fulfilling his priestly duties of burning incense. The angel told him that Elisabeth will have a child and that she is to call him John, many will rejoice at his birth, and he will be great in the sight of the Lord.

We find in Matthew 11:11, Jesus says, "Verily, I say unto you: among them that are born of a woman, there have not risen a greater than John the Baptist. Notwithstanding, he that is least in the Kingdom of Heaven is greater than he."

In Luke 1:76–79, Zachariah, filled with the Holy Ghost, prophesied over John that he shall be called the prophet of the highest! For he will go before the face of the Lord to prepare his ways, to give knowledge of salvation unto his people by the remission of their sins, through the tender mercies of God, to give light to them that sit and darkness and in the shadow of death to guide our feet into the way of peace.

In Matthew 14:1–10, John did not live for the opinions of others. John stood up against the immorality of Herod Antipas, ruler over Galilee, who took his half-brother's ex-wife, Herodias, to be his wife, which was a transgression against the Mosaic law.

Herodias had her daughter dance before Herod. He was very pleased with her performance and vowed to give her anything she wished for. Herodias put her daughter up to ask for John the Baptist's head on a platter. Many people followed John yet, he did not become proud or self-focused. John's mission was to speak truth and point others to Christ.

> He must increase, but I must decrease.
> (John 3:30 KJV)

It is not about us; it is all about Christ.

Moses, Exodus 3

Moses shepherded the sheep of his father-in-law, Jethro, for forty years. One day while leading the sheep on the backside of the desert by the mountain of God, Horeb, an angel of the Lord (Jesus) appeared to him in a flame of fire from a bush.

God called Moses to shepherd the Israelites out of the hands of the Egyptians. The angel told Moses that he saw their affliction, heard their cry, knew their sorrow, and saw their oppression from the Egyptians.

Moses immediately became self-focused, dwelling on who he is and his limitations. He said, "Who am I that I should go to the pharaoh and that I should bring the Israelites out of Egypt? Besides, I am not good with words; and even though you spoke to me, I got tongue tied." Moses pleads with God to send someone else. God allows Moses's brother, Aaron, to be his mouthpiece.

> Aaron will be your spokesman to the people, he will be your mouthpiece, and you will stand in a place of God for him, tell him what to say. (Exodus 4:16 NLT)

God saw the love Moses had for the Israelite people. He also saw leadership quality: a shepherd, protector, and provider.

God equipped Moses to shepherd the Israelites out of Egypt. It is not about being worthy or good enough; it is all about God and his purpose.

Paul, Acts 8

Paul was called Saul before his conversion (Acts 13:9). Saul made havoc of the church, entering every house and dragging men and women out, committing them to prison for their faith. He went as far as to get a letter from the high priest to enter the synagogues at Damascus so that if he found any Jesus followers, man or woman, he might bring them down to Jerusalem to be martyred.

Saul's conversion: Damascus road experience. As Saul came near Damascus, suddenly a light shone about him from heaven. Saul fell to the earth, and he heard a voice saying to him, "Saul…Saul…why persecute me?"

Saul said, "Who are you, Lord?"

The Lord said, "I am Jesus, whom you persecuted. It is hard for you to kick against the prick." This means to hurt oneself by persisting in useless resistance or protest.

The work Paul did after his conversion could not erase his past or make him worthy to be called an apostle; He could not make himself good enough outside of Christ.

> For I am the least of the Apostles and do not even deserve to be called an apostle, because

I persecuted the Church of God. (1 Corinthians 15:9 NIV)

Paul's Strategy Against Condemning Thoughts

First, Paul took every thought captive.

> Casting down imaginations, and every high thing that exalts itself against the knowledge of God and brings it into captivity every thought to the obedience of Christ. (2 Corinthians 10:5 KJV)

We must hold thoughts up to the truth of God's word, tearing down strongholds in our minds that have built themselves up against the truth. By speaking the truth, we block the lies that are trying to make their way from our minds to our hearts. Let us no longer speak the lies of self-condemning thoughts.

Second, Paul proclaimed the truth of God's word:

> I have been crucified with Christ; it is no longer I who live, but Christ lives in me, and the life which I now live in the flesh, I live by faith in the son of God, who loved me and gave himself for me. (Galatians 2:20 NKJV)

Third, Paul did not dwell on his past, including his failures and hangups.

> No, dear brothers and sisters, I have not achieved it, but I focus on this one thing; forgetting the past and looking forward to what lies ahead. (Philippians 3:13 NLT)

Fourth, Paul focused on Christ:

> But whatever I am now, it is all because God poured out his special favor on me and not without results. For I have worked harder than any of the other apostles; yet it was not I but God who was working through me by his grace. (1 Corinthians 15:10 NLT)

When we become preoccupied with our weakness, we are simply turning our attention back onto ourselves. We put ourselves in God's place when we judge ourselves.

Food for thought: Are we saying that the Holy Spirit is not competent enough to do his work of convicting us concerning sin, unrighteousness, and judgment? Are we saying, "He is not capable of doing it; we must do it for Him?"

Worthiness has nothing to do with us and everything to do with Jesus.

> Being justified freely by his grace through the redemption that is in Christ Jesus. (Romans 3:24 KJV)

> Therefore being justified by faith, we have peace with God through our Lord Jesus Christ. (Romans 5:1 KJV)

Jesus's birth, death, and resurrection made it possible for God's grace to cover our total inability to be good enough.

Fifth, Paul rests in truth, claiming friendship with God.

Paul was chosen by God:

> According as he has chosen us in him before the foundation of the world, that we should be

holy and without blame before him and love. (Ephesians 1:4 KJV)

God gave us rights to become his child:

> But as many as received him, to them he gave power to become the sons of God, even to them that believe in his name. (John 1:12 KJV)

God understands and knows me:

> Before I formed you in the belly, I knew you. (Jeremiah 1:5 KJV)

> And this was manifested the love of God toward us, because that God sent his only begotten son into the world, that we might live through him.
> Herein is love, not that we loved God, but that He loved us, and sent his son to be the propitiation for our sins. (John 4:9-10 KJV)

We are not justified by others' opinions or our own, but by the precious blood of Jesus, which leads us to our last area affected by self-condemnation.

Judgmental and Critical Spirit

Living with self-condemnation often leaves us feeling judged by others. The condemning thoughts keep replaying bad experiences and failures. We are constantly feeling the need to compare, judge, and criticize to feel superior.

Let us take a look at what God's Word says about judging and criticizing:

> Oh, don't worry; we wouldn't dare say that we are as wonderful as these other men who tell you how important they are! But they are only comparing themselves with each other, using themselves as the standard of measurement. How ignorant! (2 Corinthians 10:12 NLT)

We touched on earlier how it is not wise to lean on our own understanding (logic). We must turn to God's word for truth; our own standards may change overnight. God's word remains the same.

> Do not judge, so that you will not be judged. For in the way you judge, you will be judged; and by your standard of measure, it will be measured to you.
> Why do you look at the speck that is in your brother's eye, but do not notice the log that is in your eye? Or how can you say to your brother, "Let me take the speck out of your eye," and look, the log is in your own eye?
> You hypocrite, first take the log out of your own eye, and then you will see clearly to take the speck out of your brother's eye. (Matthew 7:1–5 NASB)

> But why do you judge your brother? Or treat them with contempt? For we all will stand before God's judgment seat. (Romans 14:13 NIV)

Have you ever wondered why others' opinions of us are so important? Have you ever found yourself obsessed over what others may be thinking about you?

Here is an example: You text a friend several times; she doesn't text back. Under false assumptions, you start to think she is mad at you. But truth be told, she had a family emergency. Amid the chaos, she forgot to call you back.

When we are focused on others' opinions of us, we are seeking their approval. We want to know that we are liked and accepted, that we measure up. How others react to us is often a reflection of what is going on in their life, their insecurities and past wounds. Most of the time, it has nothing to do with us.

When we are looking for feedback from others, we are asking them to tell us who we are. In doing so, we bring dishonor to God by relying on others' opinions to validate who we are, thereby worshipping people by seeking their approval above God's.

Seeking the approval of others

What does God's word say about seeking the approval of others?

> Thou shalt have no other gods before me.
> (Exodus 20:3 KJV)

> For do I now persuade men, or God? Or
> do I seek to please men? For if I yet please men,
> I should not be the servant of Christ. (Galatians
> 1:10 KJV)

> You adulterers and adulteresses! Do you not
> know that friendship with the world is enmity
> with God? Whoever therefore wants to be a
> friend of the world makes himself an enemy of
> God [elevate others and self]. (James 4:4 KJV)

God calls us adulterers and adulteresses because we go after other gods to appease ourselves and others to feel accepted.

> Put not your trust in princes nor in the son
> of man in whom there is no help. (Psalm 146:3
> KJV)

Do not put humans above God.

Let us now take a look at a man who sought to appease others and receive their approval and praise.

Man of God Who Sought Approval of Others

Aaron, Moses's Brother, Exodus 32

While Moses was up on the mountain receiving the Ten Commandments from God, the Israelites began to complain to Aaron, "Look, we do not know what happened to Moses, who brought us out of Egypt. Come on, make us some gods who can lead us." Notice, the people did not look at Aaron as a leader but as someone who would appease their wishes.

Aaron acceded to the people's wishes by telling them to bring to him all their gold jewelry. He took the gold, melted it down, molded it into the shape of a calf, and gave it to the Israelites. The people, discrediting the one true God, explained, "O Israel, these are the gods who brought you out of the land of Egypt!" Aaron saw how excited the people were. He took it a step further by building an altar in front of the golden calf. Then he announced, "Tomorrow will be a feast to the Lord." The people indulged in pagan debauchery (immoral behavior).

Aaron did not take a stand for the one true God. He brought glory to himself by seeking approval of others.

When Moses confronts Aaron for not taking a stand for the one true God, Aaron proceeds to blame the people: "You yourself knows how evil these people are." Aaron claimed his innocence when Moses questioned him about the golden calf. Aaron lying through his teeth said, "The people brought me the gold, and I simply threw it into the fire and out came this golden calf."

What can we glean from Aaron?

Aaron was not looked up to as a leader, but as one who succumbs to others wishes. He brought dishonor to God by seeking approval and praise from others. Aaron caused others to stumble into sin by not speaking truth.

> And Moses said to Aaron, "What did these
> people do to you, that you have brought such a
> great sin upon them?" (Exodus 32:21 NKJV)

Aaron became judgmental and critical when confronted for his lack of leadership and not taking a stand for the one true God. Aaron was self-focused and was dealing with shame, guilt, and his should have, could have, and would haves.

We must ask ourselves a very important question:

> For do I now persuade men or God? Or do
> I seek to please men? For if I yet please men, I
> should not be the servant of Christ. (Galatians
> 1:10 KJV)

> Now fear the Lord and serve him with all
> faithfulness. Throw away the gods your ancestors
> worshiped beyond the Euphrates River and in
> Egypt, and serve the Lord.
> But if serving the Lord seems undesirable to
> you, then choose for yourselves this day whom
> you will serve, whether the gods your ancestors
> served beyond the Euphrates, or the gods of the
> Amorites, in whose land you are living. But as for
> me and my household, we will serve the Lord.
> (Joshua 24:14–15 NIV)

Choose today whom you will serve. We are a servant to whom we seek approval.

Am I in Agreement with God?

We cannot walk with our creator if we are not in agreement with Him.

Can two walk together, unless they agreed? (Amos 3:3 NKJV)

Do I agree with God that I am a new creation in him, that the old ways have passed away?

Therefore, if anyone *is* in Christ, *he* is a new creation; old things have passed away, behold all things have become new. (2 Corinthians 5:17 NKJV)

God is doing a new thing in our lives.

Forget the former things; do not dwell on the past. See, I am doing a new thing! Now it springs up; do you not perceive it? I am making a way in the wilderness and streams in the wasteland. (Isaiah 43:18–19 NIV)

God has removed our transgressions from us.

As far as the East is from the West. (Psalm 103:12 KJV)

God promises not to remember our sins anymore; once they are forgiven.

> For I will forgive their wickedness and will remember their sins no more. (Hebrews 8:12 NIV)

God has a plan for each of our lives.

> For I know the thoughts that I think toward you, says the Lord, thoughts of peace and not of evil, to give you a future and a hope. (Jeremiah 29:11 NKJV)

Knowing who God is leads us to faith. God is love; he is merciful, long-suffering, righteous, and just. He cannot lie. God is immutable (unchanging). He is all powerful, all knowing, and all present. We can absolutely, confidently know that he will do what he promises.

> Trust in the Lord with all your heart, and lean not on your own understanding, in all your ways acknowledge Him and He will direct your path. (Proverbs 3:5–6 NKJV)

All glory, honor, and praise to God the Father.
Amen.

About the Author

Teresa Legates was born on November 8, 1959, in York County, Pennsylvania. She is a wife and mother of three, and grandmother of five. She is a retired truck driver of seventeen years, who has struggled with condemning thoughts, believing they were coming from a judgmental God, who was waiting to call down judgment. Finding truth in God's Word has brought freedom to her life. She presently teaches adult Sunday school. She is dedicated to early morning prayer and devotions, through which *Breaking Free from Condemning Thoughts* was born. Hearing God's call, Teresa understands that what God gives us in the kitchen is not meant to stay in the kitchen.

And he said, "Go into all the world and proclaim
the gospel to the whole creation."

—Mark 16:15 ESV